Advent

Advent

Daniel Rifenburgh

THE WAYWISER PRESS
LONDON
2002

First published in 2002 by

THE WAYWISER PRESS

9 Woodstock Road, London N4 3ET, UK

T: +44 (0)20 8374 5526
F: +44 (0)20 8374 5736

waywiser-press@aol.com
www.waywiser-press.com

Editor
Philip Hoy

© Daniel Rifenburgh

The right of Daniel Rifenburgh to be identified as the author of this work
has been asserted by him in accordance with the
Copyright, Designs and Patents Act of 1988.

All rights reserved.

A CIP catalogue record for this book is available from the British Library

ISBN 1-904130-03-8

Printed and Bound by

T.J. International Ltd.,
Padstow, Cornwall PL28 8RW, UK

for

Paola and William

Acknowledgements

"Hawthorne" and "Melville/Ishmael" appeared in *The Paris Review*; "Donald Justice Before A Soft Drink Vending Machine" appeared in *The New Republic*; "My Father's Will" appeared in *Shenandoah*; "LSD & All" and "Postlude For A Broken Marriage" appeared in *Poetry East*; "Turf Tract" appeared in *The Colorado Review*; "To My Opposite Number in Samarkand," "Major Molineux Recalls" and "Uncle Kenny" appeared in *Western Humanities Review*; "Voice" appeared in *The New Criterion*; "Andean Music" originally appeared as "Postcards of Peru" in *Southern Poetry Review*.

I wish to express my gratitude to my teachers over the years, particularly to the wonderfully robust faculty of the Humanities present at the University of Louisville during the latter half of the 1960s; to the faculty of the Department of English and the Creative Writing Program at the University of Florida during the 1980s and to the Creative Writing Department faculty at the University of Houston during the 1990s; as well as to the board of Inprint, Inc., of Houston, TX for a fellowship and to the Poetry Society of America.

Special thanks to Jean Ross Justice and Donald Justice, whose encouragement has been crucial for me, and to Richard and Doris Anita Rifenburgh, Don Flaherty, Ed Middleton Jr., and friends at the Heights Group. A tip of the hat to the "Bowery Boys" of Port Chester, New York. Finally, unsayable gratitude to those first teachers, my loving parents, William and Helen.

Regarding the above mentioned persons, I feel like that remarkable turtle glimpsed atop a West Texas fencepost: *you knew he didn't get up there by himself.*

Contents

Introduction by Richard Wilbur	13
To My Opposite Number in Samarkand	19
My Father's Will	22
Turf Tract	24
LSD & All	26
Sueño De La Guerra Generica	28
Andean Music	29
Voice	38
Melville/Ishmael	39
Hawthorne	41
Major Molineux Recalls	42
Down There	43
Postlude for a Broken Marriage	44
The Old at Hillsboro Inlet	45
Written Words, Like Paintings	47
Uncle Kenny	48
Belt	49
El Vendador	50
Suburban Song	52
My Wife at Daybreak Singing in Spanish a Psalm of Ascents	54
Socrates' World	55
Frère Villon	58
Donald Justice Before a Soft-Drink Vending Machine	59
Lycidas	60
The Demiurge on Vacation	63
Glance	67
Skip Tracer	68
Fra Giovanni	69
Sterben An Frauen	70
Homage to Henri Coulette	71
Ice House in the Rain, Georgia	78
Relapse	79

The Unicorn	80
Poem #3	81
Nativity	83
Death Poem with a Line from Vallejo	85
For Paola, In Peru	86
On a Portrait of John Keats	87
Advent	88
Index of Titles and First Lines	91
A Note About the Author	93

Introduction

Poetry has always been said to speak a charged, heightened language, and that is still part of its job description, even if some of our contemporary verse is pretty prosaic in character. Daniel Rifenburgh's words, which I first came across five years ago, seem to me to bear a considerable charge, and perhaps I can give some reasons why.

Though he can admirably sustain a sardonic mood ("El Vendador"), a comic one ("Donald Justice Before a Soft-Drink Vending Machine"), or any other, he is most remarkable in such a poem as "Turf Tract," whose truant speaker has temporarily neglected poetry for the easier excitement of betting on the horses. The poem moves fluently, and with great accuracy of tone, through a sequence of moods (including defensive mockery, irony, slangy idealism, disgust, rueful mimicry), and ends with a poignant lyric vision in which the "fleet hooves" of horses embody the beauty, striving, and brevity of life.

Such poetry is rich because of its many articulate selves, and the way its variety of voices makes for a striking texture of dictions: in Rifenburgh's "Lycidas," for instance, such a lofty line as, "And I will find again the diurnal track" is just three lines away from "Willie Boy, you beat / Me back to the barn," and both of those tones are appropriate and authentic.

Rifenburgh's poems have their linear norms, their stanza-like divisions, their reminiscences of basic meters, but what governs the movement of his poems is a genius for the speaking voice – its keys, rhythms, and modulations, its dialects and echoes. So strong and sufficient is that ability, that his poems often deal audaciously with the elements of traditional form, and get away with it. Sometimes there will be an expressive local flurry of rhyme and assonance, seeming perhaps like a brief jig or – as at the close of "LSD & All," – a muted dirge. When this poet makes use of the villanelle, as in the delightful "Written Words, Like Paintings," he takes the form over rather than strictly complying with it.

The language of *Advent* often has the force of spare accuracy: it can also stun the reader with a brilliant, slow-fuse image. Both kinds of powerful language are in this snippet from "The Old at Hillsboro Inlet," a poem in which elderly tourists are perching on a Florida breakwater and gazing at the sea.

> They seem to sit and peruse
>   Seamarks, spume
> And the beating of wings
> In the open vestibule, exhuming
> A lacquered sensitivity, wanting
> To groom themselves to the air,
>   To the sea,
> Desiring, perhaps, a practice flight
> For the leave-taking from the flesh,
> The shedding of tugged sleeves.

That splendid last line has a multiple effect. Quite apart from its meanings, it is a unique, surprising assembly of words; it serves as a figurative variation on the preceding line; its sleeves are part of the literal, windy scene; and "tugged" makes us think of how we are plucked at by all the importunities of the body and the world.

The close of that poem is particularly moving, as the reader will find, and for all his complexity Rifenburgh is a poet of strong, forthright feelings, dark or light. His feeling for poetry itself has a daring and unfashionable exaltation, and he can say, after experiencing Montale's *The Storm*,

> . . . it seems, in the afterglow of such reading,
> As if light had an enduring stepchild in the world
> Wandering between the Word and its infinite extension . . .

More than a few of Daniel Rifenburgh's lines can make you feel that way.

Richard Wilbur

Cummington, Massachusetts
September 2001

The Father is speaking work and the Son is working speech.

— Meister Eckhart

To My Opposite Number in Samarkand

You say this spring the cherry trees
Again "make light" of their burden of blossoms,
The gong inside the old Buddhist temple
Has been silent since New Year,
One great bronze ear, listening,

While the prayer calls from
The high towers of the mosques
Seem incessant, menacing the flights of sparrows,
And the lone orthodox church, unevangelistic,
Braves it out beneath its mushroom caps
With incense and candles.

That's precisely to be expected, is why,
Perhaps, you get the best tea in Trans-Oxiana
And the samovars seem to know it. Check
Marco Polo, Avicenna, or your own letter
From last year.

    Here Autumn's cranking up,
That's how late I am in answering.
There are parties somewhere, the new styles
Of automobiles are revealed, bright
Epiphanies on wheels and, for me,
School again, and the astringency
Of chalk dust on my professorial fingers.

As usual, I'm torn between two urges:
To pound the student's heads with the fat grammar book,
Repeatedly, and to have them all unclothe
And read, in flawless Tuscan, the *dolcestilnovistas,*
Neither of which course will reach fruition.

To My Opposite Number in Samarkand

                                                Once again,
It's the middle of the muddle of the
Road of life, my circuitous *curriculum vita*
And, everywhere, the slow eyes
Of the lion, the she-wolf, the leopard,
And no Virgil coughed up from Limbo
To concert the discordant jangle,
Nor put my hand in the hand of Beatrice,
That aerial Diotima.

It's times like this that I give up wavering
Between a thanatoptic Christ
And the bloodless Neo-Platonists
And declare, to no one, "Parmenides was right,
None of this exists!" and kick, *pues nada*,
The dog, or hit the bottle.

At least there's still poetry.
I've been reading Montale.
The Storm does not dazzle
But pulls you in like an undertow, with
A slow accretion of detail,
Quiet *intermezzi*, a voice
Like the sea, and again you're drowned.

You may walk around the corpse now,
Finger the blue-brown kelp clinging to the hair,
Your ghostly hips bruised by the drenched table.

Or, so it seems, in the afterglow of such reading,
As if light had an enduring stepchild in the world
Wandering between the Word and its infinite extension,
Finding play in the interstices and *lacunae*
Where even breath must pause
In its tally of declensions
And what enters then by a grace
Commands our strictest reverence.

To My Opposite Number in Samarkand

Write again, next Spring, the same letter
If you're able, and go, speak for me
Into that bronze ear, this word,
"Parmenides," and tell me if the figured Boddhisatvas
Find it pleasing.

My Father's Will

When he knew he was about to die, my father
Gathered his three sons and his brother
Around our oval, oaken table.
He handed his written will to me. Read it,
He indicated, and I began reading the thing
Aloud, groping with the first sentences.

He would have read the will himself, but the thing
That was killing him was throat cancer: it
Had seized that voice my brothers
Remembered as both bell and thunder. Charged sentences
He spoke in wrath could split a table.
We'd heard his voice as Zeus, Jehovah, God the Father.

I didn't want to read the thing
But, obedient, started in on it.
After five or six sentences
He cut me off, slamming the table.
I looked up and my father
Indicated angrily that it be passed to my eldest brother.

I supposed I had done a bad job of it
And pushed the papers across to my brother.
He got only about three sentences
Into the document when my father
Pounded his fist on the oaken table
Again, shaking the thing.

Regathering his composure, my father
Directed the will be given to his brother
And once more across the table
Went the troublesome thing.
My uncle spoke firmly from the first sentence
And was allowed to read uninterrupted to the end of it.

My Father's Will

Now, what was in it,
I don't think I remember a sentence
Of the damn thing,
Nor do my brothers.
I only recall the pounding of the table
And the rage whelming within my father.

Sitting at the same table, recalling that day, my brothers
And I speak of it in falsely casual sentences.
My father's will is still a terrible thing.

Turf Tract

In Shelley's last, unfinished poem,
In Shelley's great poem which is without closure
Because the poor poet drowned in water,
in Shelley's great "The Triumph of Life,"
The last word of which is "of"
And the whole thing stops right there
While Shelley goes out to take in a boat ride
(Talk about your Lethe and Nepenthe!),
We meet, according to Harold Bloom
And Lionel Trilling, "Rousseau,
Prophet of nature, serving
As a surrogate for Wordsworth, entering
The poem as Virgil, the guide to Shelley's Dante,"
And all of this is related to you by Rifenburgh.

It's much easier, and sometimes as rewarding,
To study the bloodlines of flat-track thoroughbreds,
Such as: *Raise A Bid* got out of *Botcha*
Botcha's Bid, or, *This
Is Enough* from *On To Glory*
Gave *This Is Glory,* especially if he won,
But *Life* always wins. It's got
By *Spirit* out *of Some Kinda Shit*
And the odds are a zillion to one
(Or, is it one to a zillion, I forget)
That Life is going to win,
Going to suck you in, and *Something Spritely*
Is the racing name of that foal.

How can you resist her?
Who said you should?

Shelley did;
Laid his pen aside for an hour
And died, gasping water for air, air
And Life.

Turf Tract

I sat in my car outside the track
And counted my losses.
Life lay down with death beside me
And they had the nerve
To fornicate in front of me.

I was thinking how *Mar Best* gave
Mon Go Fast by *Mongo*
And mon do go fast
But the colt, he finish last
And my money was wasted
Fast as life, fast as that,

Fast as was the track
Where the fleet hooves
Tossed up the turf;
The little clods of this our earth,
The quick, high flinging and falling of

LSD & All

There were several of us back there in the Sixties,
Rising on acid, blues riffs and ragas,
Who took the shorter, grand tour of Heaven

And actually returned to post-lapsarian Earth
(The joke of sheer descent
First issuing in mirth).

We found ourselves married,
Soon divorced,
Dead poems in our hands,

Some of us drafted
Into the service, given guns
To clean, shoulder,

And to shoot. I blew up
A very used car
On a tank range

At Fort Knox, Kentucky, and said, "Son,
This is back on Earth." We drilled through
That winter till our feet no longer hurt,

Accustoming ourselves to the dour infirmities
So long acquainted with *terra firma*
And heard, far off,

The musicians die, one by one,
Like birds departing
For new latitudes of the sun.

These times passed, too, for time
Has such a passing will.
Like great, slow millwheels

The decades roll.
Where the six o'clock chronicles
Appear on the screen and unscroll,

It's a cooler eye is cast now
And that music
Lies deep under the hill.

Sueño De La Guerra Generica

We air-dropped low into M.
And quickly set up our perimeter.

Inside, things grew normal:
Our laundry got done,

The food wasn't bad
And some of the camp followers were interesting.

Here night floats down like a corrupted petal
And the days bloom lush, unreal and palmy:

*Kingdoms of red, green
And yellow.*

Recon patrols come back reporting
An absence of definite fronts,

Pockets of friendlies,
Good *ganja*.

In that distant city
By a blue lake,

Nestled among blue mountains,
The peace talks drag on.

Andean Music

> *Hay golpes en la vida, tan fuertes . . . yo no sé!*
> There are blows in life, so strong ... I don't know!
> — César Vallejo, *Los Heraldos Negros*

I. *Los Tres Reyes*

This year *El Niño* crawled between the barren coast
And the cold, anchovy-bearing Humboldt, bringing,
With his blood-warm waters, floods
In the North, drought in the South
And a paucity of fish.

In Tumbes the fresh water pipes and the sewers are broken
And inextricably mixed. Cholera, diphtheria, hepatitis
And the rest of the usual diseases
Arrived with the rainclouds and linger,
Multiplying with the mosquitoes, yet

From Titicaca down to Huancayo
The crops lie stunted, withered
In the fields with thirst. It is said a child
Can be bought for ten dollars in the highland villages
And the *guerreros* of *Sendero Luminoso* roam over Ayacucho.

It's been a bad year all over the land, since Christmas,
When the farthest trawlers first felt the Infant's namesake,
The fishermen's thoughts turning quickly to dread
When they considered what gifts, *que regalos,*
The Three Kings had in their oriental heads.

II. Shine

In the Plaza San Martin in downtown Lima
A shoe-shine man snags the newly-arrived tourists
Trickling out of the splendid Hotel Bolivar.
At the end he hits them up for five bucks
In Peruvian notes, milking their confusion, but

Andean Music

Gives a great shine, spitting on their toes,
Slapping their feet like crazy.

III. Cuzqueñan Nightcap

There's not much joy in Cuzco tonight.
A lawyer named Pizarro bums a smoke off me.
Bums another smoke, I should say.
He's elegantly tailored, I'll give him that.

And where is the cigarette vendor tonight,
The shy, sissy kid with the broken smile
And American smokes? Perhaps he's tired of our money,
Perhaps he's scolding his weary legs or making
A contraband run to the border.

It doesn't matter. We'll finish this round
Then walk along the cobbled streets,
Across the fine Plaza de Armas,
To Calle Suecia on the other side of town
And lay the lungs down, wondering, only briefly,

How the old ladies, these Quechua squaws, can
Sit out on the cold streets all night, waiting
For the sunlight so they can plead, *"Compre mi champa,"*
"Buy my sweater." How do they do it? Why must they,

Like barnyard animals,
Suffer the exigencies of such weather?
Some questions get born in the brain, arise,
Only to fall back again *(Yo no sé!)*

And it is leagues and miles,
Miles and horizons — and more —
From this Andean town under the Southern Cross

Andean Music

And track of Capricorn to the country
Some here call The Monster Of The North,

My homeground, where tonight
America can go outside and look up
And see how the Dipper tilts and pours out Polaris
As if that lodestar were a stoplight or jealous magnet

For the traffic of earthly blessings
And its precincts bore no prancing of goat feet,
Only the stalk-eyed seeking and sure outward
Attenuate reaching
With the either claw of Cancer.

IV. Where The Puma Sleeps

Jorge takes me above the bowl of Cuzco,
Up into the mountains, calling out the plants,
What each is good for (sniff the delicate *muña* after
Crushing it in your fingers and the sinuses open), pointing

To where the *pumas* should now be sleeping, where the corn
Grows, that takes two summers, up here, to mature; the sacked
Tombs on the cliffside, the twin
Zig-zag troughs at Quenko, the one

In which the Incas poured *chicha,* the other
In which their virgins menstruated, the cut
Rills in the rock converging, and some aspect of the future,
By which rivulet led the way, determined.

Well, the specifics are unclear now, legend and conjecture
From an unceremonious age backward
To the old prognosticators, those who foresaw,
Plainly, the arrival of Pizarro.

. . . the poor bastard, analfabeto,
Beating it out of the failed,
Hardscrabble land, Estremadura,
With his only birthright his hunger, nerve, arms, hands.

V. To The Poet Javier Heraud

Te gusta este jardin que es suyo? Evite que sus hijos lo destruyen!
Do you like this garden which is yours? Keep your kids from destroying it!
– Malcolm Lowry, Under The Volcano

Javier, this is what the *yanqui medicos*
Call synergetic. The corporeal

Organs of the state
Have grown these salubrious thickets

Of nerves to interrelate. See
Those little wires coated

In many-colored plastic, bundled
Strands of them

Held fast by thicker wire, like flowers
In a street kid's hand,

And all the bundles
Going past you, *como los serpientes?*

Sideways they move, caduceus-charmed,
Toward distant computers

Via Comsat, ITT,
Entelperu.

Andean Music

Maimonides can't
Unperplex you, rose

Of an ear pouring blood
On the plaza cobblestones;

Milton nor St. Augustine
Explain to you, *poeta de los rios,*

Who have become your own pure river,
Falling off either cheek of the Andes:

East into the jungle
Hastening the Apurimac,

West where the Rimac
Drains the streets of Lima.

The clothes of the radio walk down
Through the Madre de Dios, shoot a poet,

Leave his liver rocking, creaking
Like an Arab dhow. They arrive

On arcs of air, unwind, do
The labor of dominion there

And disappear,
Dew misting

From the lizard's spine.
Javier, this is synergetic, see

Those little wires
Lacing the eyelets of the garden, this

Andean Music

Garden
Which is yours?

VI. *El Condorito*

The unofficial mayor of Macchu Picchu
Is a long-haired Argentine called Che Ernesto.
I met him in Aguas Calientes where he sat outside a cafe.
I stood and looked, unaccountably transfixed,

And he offered me his glass of *pisco*.
He once carried a hang-glider to the peak of Huanca Picchu
And jumped off, twirling like a wounded condor,
Everyone looking, amazed,

Till he landed upright on the slim
Bank of the raging Urubamba. The locals
Give Che whatever he wants, within means and reason.
They know he's readying himself for the next flight.

In his room we played guitars, chewed
The leaf and ate each a handful *of Cacto San Pedro,*
The nylon wings folded in a corner,
Then headed, in the dark before dawn, up to the sacred city.

VII. Vallejo, In Paris, On A Thursday, Rain

The doctors cannot discover
The cause of my dying. I tell them:
It is an unknown cause, one
You will never find, and I've always known it.

Andean Music

The cause is nothing
And nothing could ever
Have stopped being its cause.
If my life had been
Different ... still, *este nada,*
And I would die of this unknown malady:
A black pebble on a white stone.

Take from me this cup, *Mamallay,*
This taste like tungsten, like
Lagrimos de Cristo, these
Leaf-dregs of colored rotogravures

And bad history, vistas
Of tubercular cities
Pyramiding on a dry coastal plain.

Pachamamay, Mother Earth, thirsty
For tears, blood, the spongey kidneys of men,
Aparta de mi este caliz,
These sierras of grief, white
Rivers of loss
Cascading to night and exile.

Yo, César Vallejo, de
Mente sano . . . naci en Infierno
Hijo de golpes . . . de la patria Poesia,
Quedo aqui mi primer testamento:
Tan fuertes! . . . Yo no sé!

VIII.

Forty phantom jets
Sit on the tarmac
Of Jorge Chavez airport at Callao

Andean Music

Awaiting the call to defend,
From enemies without,
La patria, El Peru. Tonight
The only lights in Lima

Come from the headlights of taxis
Circulating through the streets of the capital.
The guerrillas have entered the city
And blown the electrical grid,

Felling pylons with sacks of dynamite.
The jails are full and organized by the jailed,
As are the ghettos, by the ghettoized
And the madness of the one side, the dispossessed,
Equals the madness of the other.

Above this sanguinary equilibrium
Of uncivil disorder,
Above, even, the blood of innocents
Slain in Andean villages

Soar the condors, who, if you watch them,
Are closer to vultures than to eagles.
Their ancestors picked at the carcasses,

Indiscriminately, of the Inca's men
Or Pizarro's, indifferent to whose marrow
Fed the fetid maw of battle

And the titanic walls of Sacsaywaman
Were black weeks with the black sheen of them,
Feasting.

This is the last lesson, your exit tax,
A few lines from Prescott's *History of the Conquest,*
The receipt you take aboard the *747*
As you leave Peru.

They examine your passport,
Your luggage. You are a tourist;
You may go. *Adios! Regressa!*
Here's a last shot of *pisco,* gratis.
Vuelve, Señor, otra vez
A nuestra Peru!

And you know, as you rise above
The fog of Lima, the ocean on your left,
On your right, the living, telluric mural
Of the Andes, that Atahuelpa erred
When he said, at Cajamarca,
"Without my consent, no bird
Flies through this empire."

Cuzco, Gainesville, Houston

Voice

Today I am proud of all poets everywhere,
For it's true: the voice is sacred,
Such is this mix of meaning, muscle and air.

Though they toil in private, as at solitaire,
And often wilt among the living and thrive among the dead,
Today I am proud of all poets everywhere

For they loose the stops, and what issues there
Is like a dance upon an isthmus between two sea-beds,
Such is this mix of meaning, muscle and air,

And they are its outlets, the vivid portals in air
Through which the winds of all revelations are sped,
So that today I am proud of all poets everywhere.

Some god, in his hunger to be known, pared
His desire into a pipe of flesh, and through it like a living thread
Goes this mix of meaning, muscle and air.

O Voice, rising in rage, or lifted in prayer,
Or falling silent, in despair of all that cannot be said,
Today I am proud of all poets everywhere,
Such is this mix of meaning, muscle and air.

for Richard Wilbur

Melville/Ishmael

Call it a lack;
Lacking the ability
To stop at a certitude,
To arrive at a plain of comfort,
There to make a substantial abode and
There reside, contented, with pipe and bowl.

All is flux.
The wet wars against the dry,
The cold against the hot,

Manhattan upon the Marquesas,
Fiji upon the widows' walks
Of Bedford and Nantuckett.

So Heraclitus would have it said,
But not so Jehovah, nor
His righteous folk. Still,

The way into the valley
Of the shadow of doubt
Is the way out
And back in, as from everlasting.

Or a floated plank,
Trimmed for a coffin,
Is the way,

Where a man looks for days at the sun
Overhead, and keeps the seas at their work.

He is an orphan, or a god,
And a bible would do him
Little good.

Melville/Ishmael

A trade good, he would call it;
So much calico, so many unchapleted, ruby-like
Beads.

The board he clings to
Turns by turns
Under sun and stars.

"No!"
In thunder he declares, in counterpoint,
Adrift in his disconsolate declaration, working
Out the grammar of it, exploring the fine
Largesse of it,

As the swells pass over and under
And Rachael madly,
Vainly searches out
Her lost children.

Hawthorne

This quill is a wand;
I wave it about

And box all doubt
In a high, storied redoubt.

Thus I re-route
Pandora's rout,

Let it whelm there and riot
To the mad heart's content,

A negative number scouring
Its darkest quadrant,

While my outward life, largely undescribed,
Stays calm, covert, undefiled.

This is the art that is hid,
To wildly write and quietly live,

Loosen romance
In a brazen coffer, where furies

Cascade and rage, conflagrate
Among the mind's night-lumber,

About those frail, fanciful thought-
Structures, so weirdly wrought,

Then, having kicked
Once at the insignificant embers,

To seal the lid, lightly,
With a period.

Major Molineux Recalls

That gaze, my young kinsman looking
At me in my outfit of tar
And feathers. I must have looked to him
Like some great African bird, but
With a familiar face.

The crowd was cruel enough
Yet I knew the crown I represented
Was firmly behind me, across
The blue ocean though it was.

Such consolation
As there is in duty
Every soldier knows. I knew it
Then, and was not unmanned
By the barbarous acts of the mob.

No, I held my dignity intact
Till we rounded a corner and there
Before the church stood my amazed
Kinsman. Our eyes met and locked.
Then it was he laughed, knowing
It was I there upon the cart.

After that I took ship for England,
Having no more the heart
To stay in that cruel land
Where I know not what devil works such art.

Down There

Down there, among those isles, those peoples,
Life is different, not anti-literary,
Though it's true the rates
Of illiteracy are high; but the people
Tend to be quite unliteral
In their daily exchanges, whether a litre
Of ale, a libra of flour,
Or a miniature fishing smack, put artfully
In an old rum bottle. There all
Passing banter, as the barter,
Is finely put through the netted, lingual
Fretwork of simile, metaphor, so that
It's not at all anti-literary, the people
Speak literally like poems, ambulatory
Poems, littering the air with casual, sensible
Confusions of sense, artfully
Twisting reason to contours of the flesh, the lived life
Down there, among those saffron poets,
Where life is thought to be slightly different
From what, perhaps, you thought,
And the world, after awhile, comes at you
Through their singular filter
As if all the wisdom of your own fathers
Were displayed like a fishing smack in a green bottle
And the contents of that bottle,
Held aloft and tottered
At the end of one of those sinewy arms,
Went dancing in the sun
Like a babe in a light-bathed bottle.

Postlude for a Broken Marriage

The end of it all
Is come and gone.
The curtain fell an hour ago.

Already scenery and scaffolding
Mumble in the wings like old thunder
Played out above the low hills of Louisville.

In the darkened hall,
Beneath rows of empty seats, along
Canted aisles, what strange eyes
The mice carry as they scurry over
The dropped playbills.

Out on the sidewalk, someone has stolen the town.
It is New York, Mexico City, Lima.
Across the street is a cafe,
Still open at this hour.
A woman sits there, nibbling pastry.

Farther down the street, beyond a traffic circle,
The distant glow of other marquee lights
And dim figures, lately
Ushered forth, standing under them,
Looking left and right and before.

The Old at Hillsboro Inlet

He'll shape his old course, in a Country new. – King Lear

The long breakwater
Of square-cut boulders strewn
Out from Hillsboro Inlet appears,
   This afternoon hour,
Like a strange rookery,
So many old people are on it,
So many snowbirds lately arrived,
The elder tourists from the north
Our strip of Florida receives
In the winter months, arrayed
On their purchase of rock,
All facing and gazing long at the sea.

   "God's waiting room," my mother
Laughingly calls this part
Of the Florida coast, even
Though she's sixty-five. And so
They seem to sit and peruse
   Seamarks, spume
And the beating of wings
In the open vestibule, exhuming
A lacquered sensitivity, wanting
To groom themselves to the air,
   To the sea,
Desiring, perhaps, a practice flight
For the leave-taking from the flesh,
The shedding of tugged sleeves.

   How they regard
The mangroves, desperately rooted
To the inner shore of the inlet,
Holding the land
   In clutch,
Refusing to give up
To the fluted and edged tools
Of the tide, keeping stand

The Old at Hillsboro Inlet

    Over clumps and grains
    Of the literal ground
       Of their being;
    (They regard them as homely,
    Brave children).

       A squadron of pelicans,
    Prehistoric remnants, flies over
    In perfect "V" formation, remindful,
    To the old, of bombers skirting past Dover,
    Channel-topping, headed at the Ruhr.

    In mirroring unison
    The arms of the old rise in gesture,
    Fingers pointing, arms
    Like plucked wings of birds,
       Tremulous, bare, slender,
    And the wind comes at them,
    Strong now, lifting,
       The memorial land
    Behind them becoming a blur.

Written Words, Like Paintings

Seem to talk to you as though they were bright, clever,
But if you ask them anything about what they are saying
They go on telling you just the same thing forever.

So Plato has Socrates, in the *Phaedrus,* declare
And his complaint, his words, so incisive, disarming,
Seem also to talk to you as though they were bright and clever

But neither do they avail of probing or questioning.
Frozen on the pages these ages unending,
They go on dumbly recounting the same thing forever:

That they are counters for wit, counterfeit intelligencers,
Cobalt or crimson jewels that, their facets shimmering,
Seem to wink at you as though they were smart; however,

Just once press them, why the strict typographer
Won't let them relax, respond, refine their meaning,
And they go on blithely recounting the same thing forever.

Just so, dear reader, are these lines, scribbled by a poet
Who's soon absconded, even as they go on telling,
Like a cheap plaid suit or a scene from Goya,
An unrelenting tale forever.

Uncle Kenny

Ghostly and unknown by me,
Mangled by forceps
In difficult birthing,
We send him cards, tobacco

And, for his bad birth,
Forget him as well as can be
And do not unearth
The ghost of hard birth,

The ghastly smirk of it,
The unnerving smirk (this
Is a sane family), the forced
Forceps pinched smirk,

The — 0, don't
Get hurt
In the shiny chute
Tumbling out of eternity.

You'll get strange cards
And tobacco
From your
Ghost family.

Belt

Common sense tells us
The sun goes round the earth

And the earth itself is flat.
So much for common sense, which *is,*

Coincidentally, flat, and *does* go round the earth
Somewhat like an old chastity belt, but not so tight

That it cannot be pierced here and there
By the true child of Mother Night.

El Vendedor

It is a brilliant day over Texas.
In an unzoned coastal city, flat,
Traversed by listless bayous,
I sell, from a pine clapboard shack
On a gravel lot, Oldsmobiles to Aztecs,

Mercuries to Mayans, Lincolns to the lithe
Bronzed *mojados,* those who crossed lately
A brown, shallow river
And escaped whatever lies, haunched,
Across a southern border.

It is a brilliant day over Texas,
Good for sales, they say,
And I am the salesman
As was my father before;
As was my father: *yo soy el vendedor.*

Out on the gravel lot the brown *mojados* kneel
On their haunches by the rowed vehicles,
Perhaps listening to their spirits. These
Are not the new Americans. No,

They're the old ones, *los ancianos,* returning,
And there they sit, unspeaking, fingering the white gravel
While the sibilant tires of the traffic
Roll down old Durham Road.

Es un dia brilliante sobre Tejas
And already I speak, as I must, their lingo,
For now the men rise, breaking the rude tableaux.
They reach into dusty boot tops for bankrolls
And bring me their pictures of dead, white presidents.

El Vendedor

Once the simple contract is signed and the money stowed
I will tell them they own both halves now,
If the car breaks in two
And they will laugh, as the poor always do.

It is a brilliant day over Texas,
Even birds get dazzled and lost in this sort of blue.
Why should men, or frontiers, or money, not also be excused?
Yo soy el vendedor. Quien eres tu?

Suburban Song

With the car in the drive
And the coat in the hall,

Lay he down, assembling sleep
Out of motes, out of sheep.

Inward wings the amazon parakeet,
Singing backwards its colors;

Walks the blind switchman out
With his hand jiggling the lever.

Go, drive the dream far dark, distant
Rails converging scissors-sharp,

Straight through the bow
Of the night porter's heart, through

The watch in his vest,
His breast of dead wrens,

Him solicitous
With his coats folded high,

His keys on the sleep,
His hallway of lies.

Of the morrow's maiden morning
With the rock away rolling

Let this dreamer dream nothing,
Only green lawns passing to parkland

Suburban Song

Where the sparse houses squat
Like planed alabaster,

But fewer and fewer,
Less and less,

And there a last, lost child
Pausing thoughtless over a broken plow

And the dumb sentinel birds
Silent on cool, cantilevered boughs.

My Wife at Daybreak Singing in Spanish a Psalm of Ascents

She will lift up
Her eyes, she sings,
To the mountains, to Jehova,

Where comes her succor,
Donde vendra mi succoro,
Though there are no mountains

In coastal east Texas
And the battle god
Of that wandering tribe

Has not been noticed stopping
Here of late;
Yet she,

A source, a strength
Asks of *"Ae-o-VA"*
This succor

And lifts up her eyes,
As if to mountains,
Spreading her arms

Wide to receive
As she sings
And receives

And the faltering
Day comes on, as
If beckoned by one.

Socrates' World

Is at the center of everything,
Equidistant from all extremities,
Surrounded by the heavens and cool
Aether of the empyrean.

This sphere within the cosmic sphere
Floats not on air or water
Nor rests on the backs of Titans,
Elephants, or turtles, but abides in the aether
Perhaps of contentment at being the very center.

There it exists in its equilibrium,
Round, free-standing,
Penetrated by swirling liquids and gases; chiefly,
Oceanus, father of waters, the wide-ranging
World-river circulating round Africa, Europe, Asia,

Draining all lesser rivers and diving
With their effluence into Earth's bowels;
Then, at Earth's center, or a little before,
Reversing its course, from the influence of gravity
And spurned back also by the great heat there,
Returning upward, climbing to the surface;

The waters, never wholly commingled
Within the body of Oceanus, separating out
Into their various names: Archeron,
Pyriphlegethon, Styx, Cocytus, and thence,
Their races run, Oceanus again, yet some

Pooling into underground lakes first: Styx
Into the Stygian Lake, Archeron
Into the Archerusian, these basins
Formed off the great
World-chasm, subterranean Tartarus,
The abysmal avenue of waters and souls.

Socrates' World

There at these wide basins the silent majority
Of the dead arrive for penance
And purging, the worst falling lower
Into Tartarus, but others,
Even rash homicides, eventually
Swept up with the strong, rising currents
To Archeron's lake, where they
Beg forgiveness of slain victims and
Atone for sins.

These souls, according to their natures and desires,
Return upward to the supposed
Surface of the world, and are swiftly inhaled
Into newborn bodies, human and animal, thus
Entering upon life again, and opening new eyes.

But this is not the real surface of the Earth,
For we are living at the bottom of an ocean of air,
And just as a creature living on the ocean floor
Believes he sees the sun and stars

Clearly, yet, were he to rouse himself
And pierce the surface of the waves, he would
Discover, abruptly, another world, so, above us
This ocean of air ends and the true atmosphere
Of aether begins.

Up there, at Earth's real surface,
By the languid shores of air,
Live men and others. They have
Fruitful groves and temples of the gods
In which the live gods actually dwell.

Men hear their sacred voices, their prophecies,
Commune with them face to face,
And see the sun, moon and stars
As they really are.

Socrates' World

Those eminent for the holy lives
They've led arise from Archeron
And attain these, and the even higher
Habitations above, which
I have not time to describe.

The hour is nigh for me to bathe
Before I drink the poison,
And thus save the women
The trouble of washing a dead body.

A man of sense will not insist
All these things are exactly as I've described,
But it certainly appears the spirit
Is immortal — that, to my mind,

Is right and proper for a man to risk
Believing. The chance is beautiful,
And it's fitting for him
To charm his thought
With some such minstrelsy.

Bury me any way you like, if
You can catch me
And I don't
Get away from you.

Frère Villon

Come, brother, thief, poet,
Come, let us walk these cold boulevards
And take the wintry road for St. Denis
Out into the suburbs,

There, where the burghers
Sleep in their fat beds, snoring
Behind bolted doors.

Let us wake the master
Of a prosperous house
With steel at his neck
And break bread with him.

Let us sit him in his best chair
And explain, rationally, calmly, to him
Our program for poetry, and bread.

Come, Villon, The hour is late
And these burghers need waking up.

It is 11 p.m., December tenth, 1458.

Donald Justice Before a Soft-Drink Vending Machine

He's put his two quarters in the slot
And pressed a button,
Then another
But, nothing.

Again he presses them,
Muttering, putting some muscle
Behind the heel of his hand,
The ire rising in him, finding

Its level, faltering,
Spent finally in a last muted
Jab and last muted curse, the eyeglasses
Edging further along the bridge of his nose.

He'll not kick the machine
Nor report to the office across campus
For a refund. Upstairs
The students will be reconvening

To their workshop,
Sheaves of sestinas
On the table, their own
And those of past masters before them.

For a moment he stands speechless
Before the looming, mechanical cheat,
Full in the glare of its red-blue lights, there
In the otherwise dark passageway.

The two vertical masses
Front each other, so,
Then the poet turns and heads off
Toward what he can hope to know.

Lycidas

I.

He walked out of his office one day,
Straight into a river of traffic,
Was hit by a car
And died, instanter.

Now it comes to me
To lament the death of a brother.

II.

Your later life, confused, misspent,
Is what I more lament,
And that it became this painful.

Death, after all,
Is our mother.
Quiet, regal, intent,
There is no passion in her black
Vestments, nor pity, nor lament.
She just is;
Quiet, regal, for
All our needs, sufficient.

Had you found out
Once more, how to live, still
She would have come.

She is like the floor
Dancers rise above, sometimes,
Entering a new kingdom.

All touch the ground again.

Lycidas

III.

Is death, inevitable, inevitably inviting?
Something forever calls us back to life
Till, for whatever reason, we barricade
The avenues of our listening.

Was this a dream?
I walked through those first days
Like a somnambulist, guarded by
A double-walker alongside,
His thoughts thinking in my sleeping head
Like the heard utterances of a shade.
Shyly, he steered me round from his dark direction
And walked me back this way.

Waking, I was alone on my feet, all
Trace of his thoughts past recall.
He'd calmly turned round again, now,
And my gaze was absorbed by the pall
Into which he moved, making
His measured, stately withdrawal.

Released as from a dream,
I have relearned the earth, the common light,
And I will find again the diurnal track,
The mundane ways. But

Solemn is the night,
The moon riding over.

IV.

Willie Boy, you beat
Me back to the barn

Lycidas

Out of which we were born,
Returning neither victor
Nor on a battered shield,

And leave me to paw
And puzzle on the open field
Where darkness folds bird,
Leaf and tree all around
And a blood-red sun goes down,
Red as our blood, then darkening, then gone
As the wheel of the sky goes westering on.

That you guided me back
And left me here,
I take for proof, not the lack,
That still you hold me dear

And may your calm recessional
My warrant be
Of disburdened rest
And tranquillity.

If, in that dream, I heard you right,
One day, in ripeness, or despair thereof,
The lover to the beloved's sight
Will repair, called
At last to share that feast
Which fuels and sparks the Light of light.

Till then,
Good brother, goodnight.

for W.R.R. Jr., 1943-1991

The Demiurge on Vacation

> *I divided*
> *To multitude, & my multitudes are children of care & labour.*
> — Blake, The Four Zoas

I was making ...
I loved my hands

In that stuff,
My will going forth,

A river floating
My best ideas

— So many stately yachts,
Pennanted with the flags

Of mind,
That best country.

Gradually, unwittingly,
I was taken by what must

Have been an aspect
Of waters,

(How else
Shall I say it?)

The gathering image
Of a countenance there,

The lips, nasal ridge,
Brow, eyes,

Of a grave,
Noble girl, it seemed,

A face floating
Upon the mirroring face

The Demiurge on Vacation

Of the seas,
And I, holding

The spangled, black
Make-up bag,

Highlighting
And shading

That pure, shining face
Bestowing

Definition, like
A rapt cosmetician

Or like
That sculptor

Who loved his statue
So well it spoke.

Then, altogether taken,
(Que cara

Bella)
So wrenched,

Asunder rent,
Free-falling I dropped

Into
That shining cosmos

— And one whispered
Out of nowhere

The Demiurge on Vacation

Before I sank
In the aspect of waters

And a passion
Of kisses,

"Farewell,
Narcissus."

You may catch me,
A family man now,

All four weeks in August
Sunning on this rock

By the Adriatic,
Ringed lightly

In seaweed
And shells,

Trying to recall
All this rightly

And the sandpipers
Piping, "Craftsman,

Free yourself,
Make wings."

And I know and
Know not

Who they mean,
Just as, soon now,

The Demiurge on Vacation

The children will
Insist

From where they
Sport themselves

In the fecund
Surf, "Papa,

Look at us, Papa!"
And for a moment

They will seem just someone's
Lovely children

Calling to their
Distracted parent

And for that moment
I will wonder angrily,

Where is
That thoughtless father

Who allowed
His attention so to wander?

Then I will flush with recognition
And dive again into the sea,

Kicking and hauling
The water past me

Till I reach
Those beautiful ones.

Glance

Clear, supple and sanguine,
My lady lounges on a white divan

And with a glance proves
   the unreconciled stress
That floods loins, locks lives, lifts dress.

Skip Tracer

It's 11 a.m. and I know what
He's doing.
He was late at a singles bar
Last night. The women were

Depressing, but the band was loud.
Anyway, the gin and tonic,
And, this morning, the head full of cotton.
At 9 he called my mother's house

In Florida, pretending to be a friend.
At 10, my last employer, that sod
Who, firing me,
Recommended God.

At 10:30, the electric company
Which powers that town I last saw
As amber lights in my rear-view mirror.
He's on his tenth cigarette now,

Punching his thousandth button.
He's not finding me.
I am in this poem,
Praying a prayer for him,

That he finds himself,
That we all find ourselves,
And can stand it.

Fra Giovanni

My backward brother John, fat, alcoholic,
Is often not a very nice person;
More like a morass
Of black, ante-diluvian feelings,
A stew
He nightly pours gold rum into:

Look in his eyes
And you can see it bubble and simmer
So that you almost expect his
Very next utterance to be

Not words, but a large bullfrog,
Escaping from his mouth
To the table, there to cast broadly
An extravagant blasphemy,
The *Paternoster,*
Perhaps, in perfect Latin, backwards,

Though poor, embittered brother John
Hates everything in simple, declarative English.

Sterben An Frauen

> Three men dead, Geiger, Brady and Harry Jones, and the woman went riding off in the rain
> with my two hundred in her bag and not a mark on her.
> — Raymond Chandler, *The Big Sleep*

I.

"We must die because we have known them." Die
Because they ride down
On mares of snow
Bowing in drifts
Around our house of wood. Die
Of their laughter thrilling off the rocks
Where the turned river makes its bend.
We must die of the unsayable smiles of women.

II.

Let the young man sigh to praise
Where they move through his breast,
Flushing out the dead. They float down
And pour wind sweetly in the portals of his head.
His roads wind purpling into the distance.

III.

But at the hour of sparrows wheeling
Through dusk's autumnal music
The older man shudders, is silent, wanders pathless
Through his still realm of sorrows, bowed
By that enormous, atrophied tumor
He drags filthily through the world:

A maundering, elephantine, purposeless heart.

after Rilke

Homage to Henri Coulette

Your mission, should you accept it ...
Mission: Impossible

I.

You will crisscross the country
And come back to this estuary,
A roadmap of wrinkles in your face,
And sit by the rushes and mudflats
Counting on your knuckles,
"Love, Death, Mother, Father, Son."
And crank the old calculator, mind,
Till it spills out the sums:
Now, and then:
Then, and now;
But all this is still before you,
The soiled right hand of the world
Is rising to greet you, stirring up the leaves,
And the open mouth of the night,
La luna llena, that nude,
Ivory wafer, O,
What is it calling?

II.

You will adjust eight-thousand windows,
For the breezes are important,
As well as the roofs.
A drunk under a brown fedora
On a street in Phoenix will say,
"When you're well off, you're well off"
He will not be talking to you,
Nor anyone, but you will turn right
At the corner, and fall in love.
This will not last. The drunk
Might have told you.

III.

Again there will be the woman
And when she says, "Sex,"
You shall answer, "Love,"
And when she says, "Love,"
You shall answer, "Sex,"
And when she pulls you on like a robe
You shall wear yourself out saying,
"Not this mule," and, "The kingdom of heaven,"
Till you come to own the leg
Walking out of your own mirror
And sit properly in the skin of your soul,
Beside her, in the innocence of knowledge.

IV.

One friend will raise cattle; another, hogs;
But you: poems like quickly molting toadstools
Appearing after a night of summer storm.
Of these, you must await further instructions.
The old woman at the back of her cave,
Mother Night, she's trying
To get the messages through.

Burn this one after reading: already
The enemy is on to you.

V.

You'll notice you cannot long balance
A volume of verse on a globe
But the globe will sit on the book
If first you force, with the globe, a slight depression,
An impression, well fitted to the rondure
Of the globe. This is called,
"Seating the guests."

Homage to Henri Coulette

    Now, serve up the truths,
The great truths, at the ends
Of their chains, barking,
And finish with epigrams, cake,
Champagne and wit. That,
And the moonlight, should do them and do it.

VI.

"*Pesta! Pesta!*" Sure, it's going around, and will be,
A real pestilence. Whom shall we throw
Into the bonfire? Who wears
The shirt of flame, this time, *Amore?*

Love, who wove it, *signores.*

VII.

At first you will have hope of yourself
While despairing, bit by bit, of the race;
Then you will despair of yourself

And the whole race;
Then you'll die and the race
Will not despair of, but bury you.

It will not carve effigies of your soul
On the hoods of Buicks,
It will drive to K-Mart unthinking.

These are the thoughts you will have, standing
By a river of headlights leaving Bakersfield
In the rain. The left tail-light

Of the last semi going over the hill
Will wink twice at you
Saying, "Fame, fame,"

Homage to Henri Coulette

Leaving a smudged residue
Of diesel exhaust on your lips
To mix with the August rain.

VIII.

You will peer at want ads
Till the want ads swim
As you look for fit labor.

Poet, they will hand you a shovel,
A gun, a broom,
And think it a favor.

They will fail to offer, to think to offer,
The hollow plume
Filled with the dark neck-blood of the earth

Poised above the skin
Of those sleek abdomens
Hidden within a blank page of paper.

They will not hear,
In their living or their dying,
The footsteps of a muse departing or arriving,

Nor, alone at their work,
The hue of metaphor crying.

IX.

Ten is the number of empire, fellow Romans,
(Decimos, el sistema decimal)

Homage to Henri Coulette

And ten decades hence,
Nostradamus' *Centuries* may make apparent
The lamb within the brazen pot,
The oracle speaking from Delphi,
Saint John scribbling on his lonely isle,
And mad John Clare, naked Blake, and all poets
Who prophesy without guile.

We only know here, of these states, meanwhile,
Whitman was dead wrong, *camerados,*
And the ravening Beast, the gaunt she-wolf
Treading the pellucid pages of the world

Turns and reads us, and the self, too well.

X.

On the morning after
The night of shattered glass,

The Weimar Yiddishers
Swept up the crystal splinters,

Put them in dustbins, boarded up
The new, too transparent vacancies,

And watched as an old man with a brush
Drew David's star on the bare lumber.

In the alluvial winter months
You will sit awhile in South American bars

With former German soldiers, drinking beer,
And the first thing each will say

Homage to Henri Coulette

Will be, "I couldn't believe we lost."
And the second thing will not matter.

XI.

Outside, in the blackness, the tip of the Lesser Bear
Will be just visible in the north,

But not Polaris. You will turn around, looking
Where the Southern Cross

Hangs like a sword
Above the antipodal ice

And think if Michael, archangel,
Plays a part in our sanguinary story

Or what shapes our fine-hewn ends
Begins and ends in what's once given,

Nature and Mind forever stranded
Through all duration and extension,

To no original, living light reflecting
Glory.

For answer, you will not return
This night to God, smitten,

But to earth
And arts of endurance:

How to tease mute hopelessness
Out of a breast still fit for singing,

Homage to Henri Coulette

To hollow out of despair
A space for the lines that might come,

And if, under a sunless wood
Where the way is lost,

There is no discrete Hell, still
You may trek the sad halls you know and aspire

To the edge
Of that pruning fork

Held like a question mark
In a hand of purgatorial fire.

XII.

Pray then that through the dark wood
Stumbles your ink-stained double agent, Henri,

A little sauced on jungle juice,
Full of talk, maps, codebooks and tobacco,

Corporal
Coulette,

Puzzling by lantern-light late
Dispatches,

The news straight from dusty
Camp Hades.

Note: This poem contains phrases from the work of the poet it seeks to honor.

Ice House in the Rain, Georgia

You can see,
Inside, the men swig their beers
And lean against the bar
As against their despair,

Pressing their elbows there
Till the joists of the flooring,
The foundation, and the red
Clay itself, must bear
Up heavily against them.

The shingled roof
That keeps them dry
Divides and sheds a drizzling,
Torporous sky,
While outside, only

A blue-tick hound, remanded
To the littered bed of a pick-up truck,
Guards the guidon of duty
In the cold rain, deaf
To the thought of giving up.

Relapse

Now,
Now is no good, I think,

And lingers on unconscionably long,
Staring down faith, while patience blinks.

Change
It up someway: a new

Roll of the dice,
A fresh quarter in the slot.

Then snake-eyes become boxcars,
Bananas become cherries.

Things may not get better,
But they'll be different.

It's not wanted or needed, to put tumbling
Dice to the boards, or slide

Two bits in the whirring machine.
Merely put the drink

Into the man.
Neat.

Now,
Now, swing your doors,

You old trickster,
Pal. Now.

The Unicorn

It is the chalice of all essence
Because it does not exist. Because it cannot be,
It owns the purest of being.

We stumblers
Between moonlight and shadows
Are offering to it the merest contingency

That it might exist,
The rough salt we proffer, with which
We tease it, withhold, and, unable thus

To coax it forth
From its dark nook in the green forest,
Feed unto our too-contingent selves.

Ah, lord of the rare beasts, of the pounded salt,
That we might, improbably,
Be,

That where a dry twitching stirs
Among dry leaves
Might that uncombed mane,

Those prancing hooves, the magic
And sportive
Great horn,

Present themselves
Our swift,
Companionable steed ...

after Rilke

Poem #3

Poem #3, the third in a series of three,
The first two of which are unwritten.

It stands in shade or sun
And presses its nose against the atmosphere,
Leans on brick walls in other people's neighborhoods,
Sending their kids for sodas and cigarettes,
Cutting louvers in the manhole covers.

The more suspect thing: a tube
Said to be connected to a needle
Pressed deep into its spleen
Through which pour all memory, rain
And unwrittenness of poems #1 and #2.

Some say it's an aqueous solution
Flowing through that flexible tube, that clear tube.
It is the very color of memory, they say,
But poem #3 refuses to turn around.

Who should be allowed to peer
Around that stout chest and look?

Only winds, roaches
And the gap-toothed children, those
Who ten minutes ago saw Clytemnestra
Whacking cabbage in their housing-project kitchen.

Out of alleys they move.
Round the corners they come.

They observe the strength drawing in,
The color or tint of it, its viscous flow
And, behind him, where you cannot go,
See the drained corpse of poem #1,
The dying hour of poem #2,

Poem #3

Their saintly visages, Christ-like and still legible, slowly
Fading through the vellum morning
To erasures, mute tracings, ghostly writhings beneath
The bold palimpsest.

For Charles Wright

Nativity

I. February

Cuando yo dare aluz mi bebe...

Dying day, slant sun,
My wife pregnant, asleep,
With small bones tying together
In her womb.

My mortality seems now and
Suddenly more tragic, not less.
Was this what I desired,

To pay more attention to life
— All piteous events, pathos itself
Amplified? The white noise of it
Keeping me up through the night?

And what of these dark commotions
Of the spirit, as if, on the bed,
A winged being between us
Wrestles itself
Through to arrival?

II. August

Now the rondure of earth
Makes a fine sphere of heaven
And the pressing life of our lives
Makes of death's looming quietude
Second skin: this boy, this son.

III. October

Given now to the light, there
I see my own image reflected
In his dark eye. That image
Will print, fix there, tarry
Where I cannot follow

As my father's image plays
Round my vision, even now,
My gaze pouring back into my son's,
Cascade

Of gaze down
Numberless
   ledges
     cascading. . .

Death Poem with a Line from Vallejo

Gods wander
Through us,
  Forceful,
  Hungering,

Spooking animals and ourselves through our glances,
Our gestures, arch over the skies of our souls
  And drop like thunderbolts
  Through us,

Falling and toeing some nitrogenous mark on the boards
Where they turn and deliver their simple lines, a word:
  "Love," "Fear," "Beauty,"
  "Death," "Anger,"

Deliver these and the Blows of tragic force,
Those which turn us out, at last,
  Of their gimcrack,
  Trompe L'oeil theatres...

Out to wet streets where the wayward pilgrims
Of some once-adored faith that Destiny has blasphemed
  Hold out to us loaves baked with
  The ashes of their losses,

And of our losses, together mixed,
That will have to nourish us on the cold journey
  That begins now
  In earnest.

For Paola, in Peru

with a fragment of a psalm

A first-ripe fig,
Ripe before summer:
When a man sees it, he eats it up
As soon as it is in his hand.

Paola, my vision reaches
Toward that band
Of stars we both can see, though
The wide world prevents us from feasting.

In July, in Cuzco,
I will meet you.

On a Portrait of John Keats

The nose is not as fine
As it might have been
If Cellini had been the sculptor,
Or Michelangelo.

One learns to look past it
To the eyes. Notice
The attitude of the head
Pausing upon the fisted knuckles

Of the one hand, at the end of the right arm,
The elbow of which sits upon
A deal table as
The poet gazes

Placidly off into life and death.
Consider

What those eyes saw,
What thoughts
Were entertained by that
Fine head,

And the feeling heart, connected
To it all, pouring stanzas out
Onto the page, which were
Pulled out of

Where? Notice the hair curling
Round those shapely ears
And the head deciding

What, of all heard things, or unheard,
It shall hear.
If you could go
Into his listening,

You would.

Advent

Rain continuous, all day
The drumming on sere leaves
That score the ground, curling
Upon nothing. They all fell, it seemed,
In a day, a day of wind without rain,
A blue norther, high pressure and
Crisp air, and the heads of the oaks
Went suddenly bald, and elm

And sycamore, all swiftly
Exposed, skeletal, gothic as Poe,
The *Materia materna* of nature
A ruined House of Usher, mad
For desolate absolutes, and now
The drear tattoo of the sky's ablutions
Syncopates the rude undress.

The mind, too, sheds a tattered cloak
And recalls elements of the old story:
The hoop round the omphalos of Christ, Marian,
The cold coin imprisoning Caesar,
A tocsin of alarm dilating the pupils of Herod,
And now the heart shunts the oil
Of incarnation out of its chambers again
In time with the last drumbeats of the rain.

We defeat the world through surrogates, and but briefly,
While placid beasts feed in drizzling pastures,
Building strength for the flight into Egypt,

Yet the son must be born in us, says the Father,
Or wither, when new oil floods the ventricles
And we become, however briefly, His surrogates
Or betrayers.

       And for this, in Winter's dead zero,
We must sing, sing Hallelujah.

Index of Titles and First Lines

A first-ripe fig	86
ADVENT	88
ANDEAN MUSIC	29
BELT	49
Call it a lack	39
Clear, supple and sanguine	67
Come, brother, thief, poet	58
Common sense tells us	49
DEATH POEM WITH A LINE FROM VALLEJO	85
DONALD JUSTICE BEFORE A SOFT-DRINK VENDING MACHINE	59
DOWN THERE	43
Down there, among those isles, those peoples	43
Dying day, slant sun	83
EL VENDADOR	50
FOR PAOLA, IN PERU	86
FRA GIOVANNI	69
FRÈRE VILLON	58
Ghostly and unknown by me	48
GLANCE	67
Gods wander	85
HAWTHORNE	41
He walked out of his office one day	60
He's put his two quarters in the slot	59
HOMAGE TO HENRI COULETTE	71
I was making ...	63
ICE HOUSE IN THE RAIN, GEORGIA	78
In Shelley's last, unfinished poem	24
Is at the center of everything	55
It is a brilliant day over Texas	50
It is the chalice of all essence	80
It's 11 a.m. and I know what	68
LSD & ALL	26
LYCIDAS	60
MAJOR MOLINEUX RECALLS	42
MELVILLE/ISHMAEL	39
My backward brother, John, fat, alcoholic	69
MY FATHER'S WILL	22
MY WIFE AT DAYBREAK SINGING IN SPANISH A PSALM OF ASCENTS	54
NATIVITY	83

Now	79
ON A PORTRAIT OF JOHN KEATS	87
POEM #3	81
Poem #3, the third in a series of three	81
POSTLUDE FOR A BROKEN MARRIAGE	44
Rain continuous, all day	88
RELAPSE	79
Seem to talk to you as though they were bright, clever	47
She will lift up	54
SKIP TRACER	68
SOCRATES' WORLD	55
STERBEN AN FRAUEN	70
SUBURBAN SONG	52
SUEÑO DE LA GUERRA GENERICA	28
That gaze, my young kinsman looking	42
THE DEMIURGE ON VACATION	63
The end of it all	44
The long breakwater	45
The nose is not as fine	87
THE OLD AT HILLSBORO INLET	45
THE UNICORN	80
There were several of us back there in the Sixties	26
This quill is a wand	41
This year El Niño crawled between the barren coast	29
TO MY OPPOSITE NUMBER IN SAMARKAND	19
Today I am proud of all poets everywhere	38
TURF TRACT	24
UNCLE KENNY	48
VOICE	38
We air-dropped low into M.	28
"We must die because we have known them." Die	70
When he knew he was about to die, my father	22
With the car in the drive	52
WRITTEN WORDS, LIKE PAINTINGS	47
You can see	78
You say this spring the cherry trees	19
You will crisscross the country	71

A Note About the Author

Daniel Rifenburgh was born in Elmira, New York on May 24, 1949. He attended the University of Louisville and subsequently served three years in the U.S. Army during the Vietnam War. He received a B.A. from Florida Atlantic University in 1981 and worked for a time as a newspaper reporter and traveled throughout Latin America. In 1987 he earned an M.A. from the University of Florida. He pursued Ph.D coursework in Creative Writing at the University of Houston and in 1996 received the Robert H. Winner Award from the Poetry Society of America, given, "to honor a poet in mid-life who has not been recognized." His work has appeared in *The New Criterion, The Paris Review, The New Republic, Poetry East, Shenandoah, Western Humanities Review,* and elsewhere. He is married and the father of a teenage son and currently resides in Houston, Texas, where he works as an adjunct college instructor and cab driver.